Denali National Park and Preserve

By Andromeda Romano-Lax

Alaska Geographic Association
Anchorage, Alaska

Alaska Geographic Association thanks Denali National Park and Preserve for their assistance in developing and reviewing this publication. Alaska Geographic works in partnership with the National Park Service to further public education and appreciation for national parks in Alaska. The publication of books, among other activities, support and complement the National Park Service mission.

Author: Andromeda Romano-Lax
Photography: Chris Byrd, 30; Jerryne Cole, 49; Michael Collier, 12; © Patrick Endres/AlaskaPhotoGraphics.com, cover, ii-iii, 4-5, 6, 7, 16-17, 24-25, 34, 39, 40-41, 42-43, 44, 52, 53, 56-57, 58-59; Fred Hirschmann: 8, 9, 10, 19, 33, 55 inset, upper right & lower left; © Ron Niebrugge/wildnatureimages.com, iv, v, vi-1, 2-3, 22, 23, 29, 32, 37, 38, 50, 51, 55 inset, lower right, 57 inset, upper & lower right; Lisa Oakley, 36; Nadja Roessek, 54-55; Gerry Reynolds, 18, 21, 26-27; National Park Service, 13, 20, 45, 48; Fabrice Simon, 57 inset, lower left; University of Alaska, Fairbanks, 46: Charles Sheldon Papers, Series 5 (Accession #76-42-4), Box 5, Folder 20, Archives, Alaska and Polar Regions Collections, Rasmuson Library, University of Alaska Fairbanks, 47: Agricultural Experience Station Album #5, 68-4-455, Archives, Alaska and Polar Regions Collections, Rasmuson Library, University of Alaska Fairbanks; John Warden/AlaskaStock.com, 14-15
Illustrations: Denise Ekstrand
Park Map: National Park Service
Designer: Chris Byrd
Editor: Nora L. Deans
Project Coordinator: Lisa Oakley
National Park Service Coordinator: Marisa James

Alaska Geographic is the official nonprofit bookstore, publisher, educator, and supporter of Alaska's parks, forests, and refuges. Connecting people to Alaska's magnificent wildlands is at the core of our mission. A portion of every book sale directly supports educational and interpretive programs in Alaska's public lands. Learn more and become a supporting member at www.alaskageographic.org

810 East Ninth Avenue
Anchorage, AK 99501
www.alaskageographic.org

Library of Congress Cataloging-in-Publication Data
Romano-Lax, Andromeda, 1970-
Denali National Park and Preserve / by Andromeda Romano-Lax. -- 1st ed.
p. cm.
ISBN 0-930931-73-4
1. Denali National Park and Preserve (Alaska) 2. Natural history--Alaska--Denali National Park and Preserve. I. Title.
F912.M23R66 2010
979.8'3--dc22
2005030611

ISBN: 978-0-930931-73-5

Printed in China on recycled paper using soy-based inks.

Wilderness in Motion

DENALI NATIONAL PARK and PRESERVE

Contents

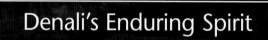

Denali's Enduring Spirit

The wolf ... reminds us of what we cannot forget: that our origins are out there, in the cold, windy outback of time, and that we are, despite all of the tinsel and trappings of civilization, still very much a part of that wild nature.

— John A. Murray

Mile after mile, the wolf lopes steadily along ridge and river bar and caribou track. Its wide paws soundlessly strike the ground. Its lanky white legs flash as it moves, then disappear into brushy shadows. Head low, apparently unhurried, it scans glacier-carved valleys and dark rising hills, searching out not one place or one kind of prey, but an opportunity: weakness, frailty, or disease. In its daily travels of up to 50 miles or more, it will fail often, bringing down prey only one attempt in ten.

It may come as a surprise, in a landscape as untouched as Denali National Park and Preserve, but wilderness can be pristine without being plentiful. In contrast with Africa's Serengeti and other lower-latitude game lands, Denali is a land of widely dispersed resources, across which animals must travel far and endure much. The wolf, like its prey, survives only by a narrow margin in this Subarctic realm, and that margin expands or contracts according to its movements. And so the wolf lopes onward, "fed by its feet," as the Russians say.

An emblem of steady energy, the wolf is rivaled only by its main prey, the caribou. These two species maintain a perpetual dance of approach and avoidance, over a six-million-acre park that is itself constantly moving, shaped by water and wind, changing temperatures, and even the colossal motions of tectonic plates.

The predator-prey movements of wolf and caribou are one kind of dance that takes place across this dynamic landscape. There are others. Often, the leading partner is not another animal species, but the swing of seasons. Days lengthen and birds answer the call by migrating polewards. The soil warms and low carpets of wildflower-studded tundra explode into color. Days shorten and the pika hurries to line its burrow with dried grass. Some of these paired motions are quick as a blur. Others are too slow to observe except with time-lapse photography. But all serve a single function: survival. And all are shaped by the specific and sometimes extreme conditions of a Subarctic ecosystem.

To understand such an ever-changing place requires motion, too—including lots of old-fashioned footwork. Between 1939 and 1941, pioneering park scientist Adolph Murie studied the tireless wolf, and proved indefatigable himself—once watching a wolf family for 33 hours straight. All that endurance might have been for naught if Murie's ideas had been rigid. At the time, wolves had reputations as rapacious scoundrels, best eliminated. Murie's findings challenged that view.

Wolves continue to excite passions within our society. They are subject to intense hunting pressure by some and viewed with awe by others. Park biologists continue the work begun by Murie which promotes an ecosystem perspective that favors relationship and connections over the success of any singular species.

Every year brings new studies proving how many connections exist—both within Denali National Park and Preserve, and between Denali and the rest of the world. The park is special because it is large enough and healthy enough to support those intact connections.

Beyond the ecological level, Denali relies upon another connection, too—the one that exists between visitors and the park. Hundreds of thousands of visitors travel the Park Road every year, hoping to catch a glimpse of a wolf, to revel in wide-open landscape views, to see the world as it might have looked when it was younger —and hopefully, how it will still look when it is a good bit older. They return home as optimistic ambassadors, energized by the knowledge that wilderness endures.

Rising Mountain, Rushing Rivers: Geology

The south side of the Alaska Range is less visited and more densely vegetated than the range's drier north side.

As we gazed a mass of clouds hanging over what appeared to be the center of the range broke and revealed two majestic peaks, Mount McKinley and Mount Foraker, glistening in the slanting rays of the afternoon sun. Far above the crest line they towered, enormous mountains, even at a distance of 120 miles.

— Alfred Brooks, USGS geologist, 1902

Kahiltna Glacier

Denali glaciers cover one million acres, or one-sixth of the park. Kahiltna Glacier on the south side of the Alaska Range is the park's longest. It originates on the south flanks of Mount McKinley and sprawls for 44 miles. Most climbers tackle the continent's highest peak from a base camp on Kahiltna Glacier, at 7,200 feet.

One cold day in 1995, Mark Stasik and Daryl Miller left their homes in downtown Talkeetna, pointed their skis and gear-filled sleds northwest toward Denali National Park, and trudged into the history books.

Over 45 days, Stasik and Miller, a park ranger, skied, and snowshoed 350 miles around Mount McKinley and its sprawling neighbor, Mount Foraker. They traveled through dense boreal forest and crossed four mountain passes. They survived a fall through river ice and other brushes with near-disaster, including a tent fire and three days without food or fuel. Without ever stepping foot on the mountain's highest reaches, they nonetheless accumulated an estimated 60,000 feet in gained and lost elevation—the equivalent of three vertical McKinleys.

Not since 1903 had an expedition succeeded in circumnavigating the Mount McKinley and neighboring Foraker massifs. Never had the feat been accomplished in winter—and certainly not by locals starting and ending an unmotorized trip from their own front doors.

Each year, more than a thousand climbers attempt to tackle the continent's highest peak. Typically, those adventurers fly to a glacier base camp at 7,200 feet. From there, it's an inclement trek of 16 miles and 13,000 vertical feet to the ice-clad mountain's summit—accomplished, on average, in about 18 days.

In other words, most adventurers choose to "conquer" the mountain by going up. (About half of them succeed.) Rare are the adventurers who experience Denali's massive majesty—and multi-faceted, geologically and climatically complex nature—by going around.

And no wonder. To circumnavigate the Denali massif is to realize that the Alaska Range has two very different faces, not easily tackled in a single season. The Alaska Range, a 600-mile arc of mountains bisecting the park, is a barrier to storms sweeping inland from the North Pacific. It catches rain, snow, and ice, which nourish the south side's larger trees and compact over time into the south side's massive glaciers: the Ruth, Tokositna, and Kahiltna glaciers, to name a few. By comparison, the north side of the range—location of the Denali Park Road and destination for all but a few summer visitors—is dry. It features less vegetation, less glaciation, and shallower, braided rivers.

From the trekker's perspective, summer presents the more favorable season for tackling the Alaska Range's dry north side. But in summer, the south side of the range—wetter and brushier—is nearly impenetrable. Winter, the more logical time to brave the Alaska Range's south side, nonetheless exposes the traveler to "unfriendly" conditions, such as the 60-below temperatures and 100 mile per hour winds experienced by Miller and Stasik in 1995.

Denali National Park is more than its famous mountain. And as Miller and Stasik's epic ski trip demonstrates, the mountain itself is far more than its frequently cloud-wreathed top. It is a massif encompassing numerous habitats and straddling two quite different climatic zones. The mountain and its surrounding park sit on another kind of dividing line, as well: the ancient meeting place of two massive tectonic plates. This boundary is fundamental to the mountain's very existence, as well as the park's most jarring recent movements.

Ancient Origins

The Earth's crust is composed of about 12 major plates. Since at least 300 to 500 million years ago, northward movement of one of these, the Pacific plate, has collided with, uplifted, and crumpled the North American plate. Today, these two plates meet at the bottom of the Aleutian Trench, off the southern coast of Alaska. But in Early Paleozoic times, this convergence boundary was located possibly as far inland as today's Park Road.

Once an ancient shoreline, today's park "moved" inland as southern Alaska took shape and was gradually enlarged by the deposition of many slivers of land, often from disparate locations. Through the movement of the Pacific plates, these mismatched pieces of land, called exotic terranes, traveled north, where they were docked or scraped off the Pacific plate as it subducted beneath the North American plate. This conveyor-like process explains why today's park is home to mixtures of rocks from diverse and distant places, including volcanic islands and the ancient ocean floor.

The collision zone where the Pacific plate meets and plunges beneath the lighter North American plate is a place of transformation. Sedimentary rock that sinks as the result of plate subduction finds its way to the Earth's hot interior, where it liquefies into a new and dramatically Earth-shaping material. About 56 million, and again 38 million years ago, tectonic activity caused this magma to rise and cool beneath the Earth's surface, forming the granitic plutons that make up

"The Mountain"

Athabascan Indians provided the name that most Alaskans use today when referring to the continent's tallest mountain: Denali, "The High One." Mount McKinley is the peak and massif's official name, however. A prospector named William Dickey named the mountain after candidate (later, president) William McKinley, champion of the gold standard. Attempts to discard the mountain's official name in favor of its more popular and ancient moniker have failed so far in Congress, but continue to be made.

the high, hard core of Mount McKinley and some of its tall neighbors. Also around this time, volcanic magma and ash spewed about the Earth's surface, creating the bands of brightly colored rocks visible from the road at Polychrome Pass.

Mount McKinley's most dramatic period of uplift seems to have taken place during the last five to six million years. And it's not over. The northward movement of the Pacific plate continues even today, with Mount McKinley gaining about one inch every 25 years. That growth may seem modest, but over time it has propelled Mount McKinley high enough to create its own weather. Battered by high-altitude cold and wind, and frequently adorned with clouds, the mountain is generally visible an average one day in three during the summer.

Elemental Architects

Just as mountains are made, they are eroded and reshaped by the elements. The most powerful and beautiful of these is water. North of the Alaska Range, valleys glisten with braided rivers. These shallow, many channeled rivers are heavy with rocks and silt eroded from their alpine headwaters. They meander across their streambeds, leaving wide stretches of gravel bar exposed. When silt blocks a channel, the rushing water carves a new course. In this way, the silver rivers epitomize Denali's restless energy.

Glaciers are called "rivers of ice." Like many unshakably true clichés, this one lays emphasis where it belongs—on the glaciers' essential quality of movement. Glaciers are created where annual snowfall exceeds snowmelt, a condition consistently met on the Alaska Range's south face. At high altitudes, in a world of perpetual winter, accumulation continues—and with it, transformation. Over time, snow becomes ice, and ice as we know it transforms from the stuff of cubes and skating rinks into even denser, bluer, glacier ice. The force of gravity obliges this surprisingly plastic substance to move

Kantishna Gold and Personalities

Denali's diverse geology includes that valuable mineral—gold—which has caused flurries of excitement all over Alaska. The mining area of Kantishna got its start in 1905 when Joe Quigley and Jack Horn staked claims along Glacier Creek, sparking a stampede of 2,000 to 3,000 prospectors. One year later, only 50 miners remained, and among these only a handful became year-round residents of the little community at the end of today's Park Road, mining not only gold, but also silver, lead, zinc, and antimony while enduring the difficulties of remote camp life.

Reflecting on these pioneers' characters, park historian William E. Brown wrote, "All of the early travelers remarked of the miners that they were a special breed, men and women of everlasting hope." And not only hopeful, but hospitable, too. Climbers, geologists, and other wayfarers often called on legendary Kantishna residents Fanny and Joe Quigley. Visitors were surprised to find a spotless home, flourishing garden, and well-stocked cellar overseen by a rifle-toting hostess who was as tough and wilderness savvy as any of the men.

downhill. On the surface of the Ruth Glacier, this slow flow has been measured at a rate of about three feet per day. Where glacier ice flows over an obstruction, or around a steep corner, large cracks called crevasses may form.

Erratic

A lonely boulder called an "erratic" was deposited at this spot long ago by glaciers—constantly moving rivers of ice that continue to sculpt the land.

In the last 10,000 years, most of the northern park's major glaciers have retreated to their high, cold cradles in the Alaska Range. But there are exceptions. The Muldrow Glacier runs northeast from Mount McKinley, makes a peculiar dogleg turn, and ends at the McKinley Bar, not far from the Eielson Visitor Center. Its dirty terminus makes the glacier easy to overlook. A thick layer of rock, soil, and rooted alder obscures the glacier's white bulk, giving the Muldrow Glacier an earthy look. But the Muldrow is indeed composed of densely compacted, multi-year ice. And like all glaciers, it moves—sometimes slowly, and sometimes at a gallop. In 1956, the Muldrow Glacier surged forward for a total of four miles, bulldozing with a vengeance up to 1,100 feet per day before it returned to relative dormancy in 1957.

While sparkling white glaciers might be hard to find close to the Park Road, their progeny are visible everywhere. U-shaped valleys, like the one south of the Savage River checkpoint, were carved by glaciers. Large boulders that look out of place, surrounded by miles of flat tundra, are called erratics. First bulldozed by an advancing glacier, they were left behind when the mighty river of ice retreated. Kettle ponds mark the spot where a large chunk of glacial ice formed a depression and, upon melting, filled it. All these features remind us that the Denali landscape was shaped over millennia, and is changing still.

The adventurous circumnavigators that opened this chapter demonstrated that humble movements, over time, can yield substantial results. Two humans, pulling heavy sleds, can encircle even the earth's grandest features. Likewise, the uplifting movements of the Earth—even as modest as a millimeter a year—can create those grand features. Equally humble elements—a drop of water, a condensed snowflake—can join forces to wear them away. Like Stasik and Miller's trip, the formation of any landscape is a dynamic and circular process, demonstrating the enduring spirit that moves both mountains and men. ■

Dinosaurs in Denali

Scientists long suspected that dinosaurs once roamed today's Denali National Park, but only in the last decade have world-class fossil finds provided the evidence. In the summer of 2005, geology students from the University of Alaska found the first dinosaur footprint in the sandstones of the Cantwell Formation along Igloo Creek. That footprint was of a medium-sized theropod, a carnivorous dinosaur that has been identified by fossil evidence in other locations in Alaska. Since that original find, new trace fossil finds include footprints of hadrosaurs, ceratopsians, pterosaurs, and several avian species, as well as body prints, coprolites (fossil excrement), fish fin traces, crayfish burrows, and many insect traces. The pterosaur finds are particularly significant, extending the northern latitude distribution of these flying reptiles.

Dating from about 65 to 100 million years ago, these faunal traces—coupled with frequent fossil plants such as conifers, shrubs, ferns and horsetails—provide evidence of a warm, biologically rich environment in Cretaceous Alaska. The dinosaur and other trace fossil assembly found so far in Denali may represent the best record of the Cretaceous ecosystem of any national park, or for that matter, any other location in the world. The dense concentration of both flora and fauna in portions of the Cantwell Formation provides ideal grounds for continued paleontological research, and a brand-new legacy of resource protection for management of Denali National Park and Preserve.

McKinley Mountaineering Timeline

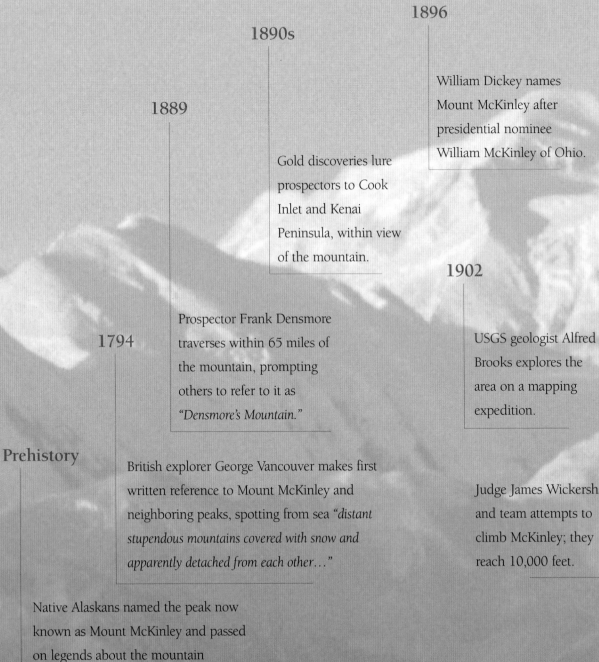

1896

William Dickey names Mount McKinley after presidential nominee William McKinley of Ohio.

1890s

Gold discoveries lure prospectors to Cook Inlet and Kenai Peninsula, within view of the mountain.

1910

Billy Taylor and Pete Anderson of the four-member Sourdough Expedition—all local novices—successfully climb the north peak, planting a 14-foot spruce pole on top.

1889

Prospector Frank Densmore traverses within 65 miles of the mountain, prompting others to refer to it as *"Densmore's Mountain."*

1902

USGS geologist Alfred Brooks explores the area on a mapping expedition.

1903

1794

Judge James Wickersham and team attempts to climb McKinley; they reach 10,000 feet.

Dr. Frederick Cook and team reach 11,300 feet and circumnavigate the mountain. Three years later, Cook claims to reach the top—a claim later disputed.

Prehistory

British explorer George Vancouver makes first written reference to Mount McKinley and neighboring peaks, spotting from sea *"distant stupendous mountains covered with snow and apparently detached from each other…"*

Native Alaskans named the peak now known as Mount McKinley and passed on legends about the mountain through their oral tradition.

1913

First ascent of the south peak by Hudson Stuck, Walter Harper, Harry Karstens, and Robert Tatum.

1947

Barbara Washburn becomes first woman to summit.

1967

Art Davidson, Dave Johnston and Ray Genet make first winter ascent.

1988

Vernon Tejas is first solo climber to summit in winter and survive.

1995

Merrick Johnston, 12, is youngest female to reach summit.

Toshiko Uchida, 70, is oldest female to reach summit.

2001

Galen Johnston, 11, is youngest male to reach summit.

2004

Mario Locatelli, 71, is oldest male to reach summit.

The Swing of Seasons: Climate and Plant Life

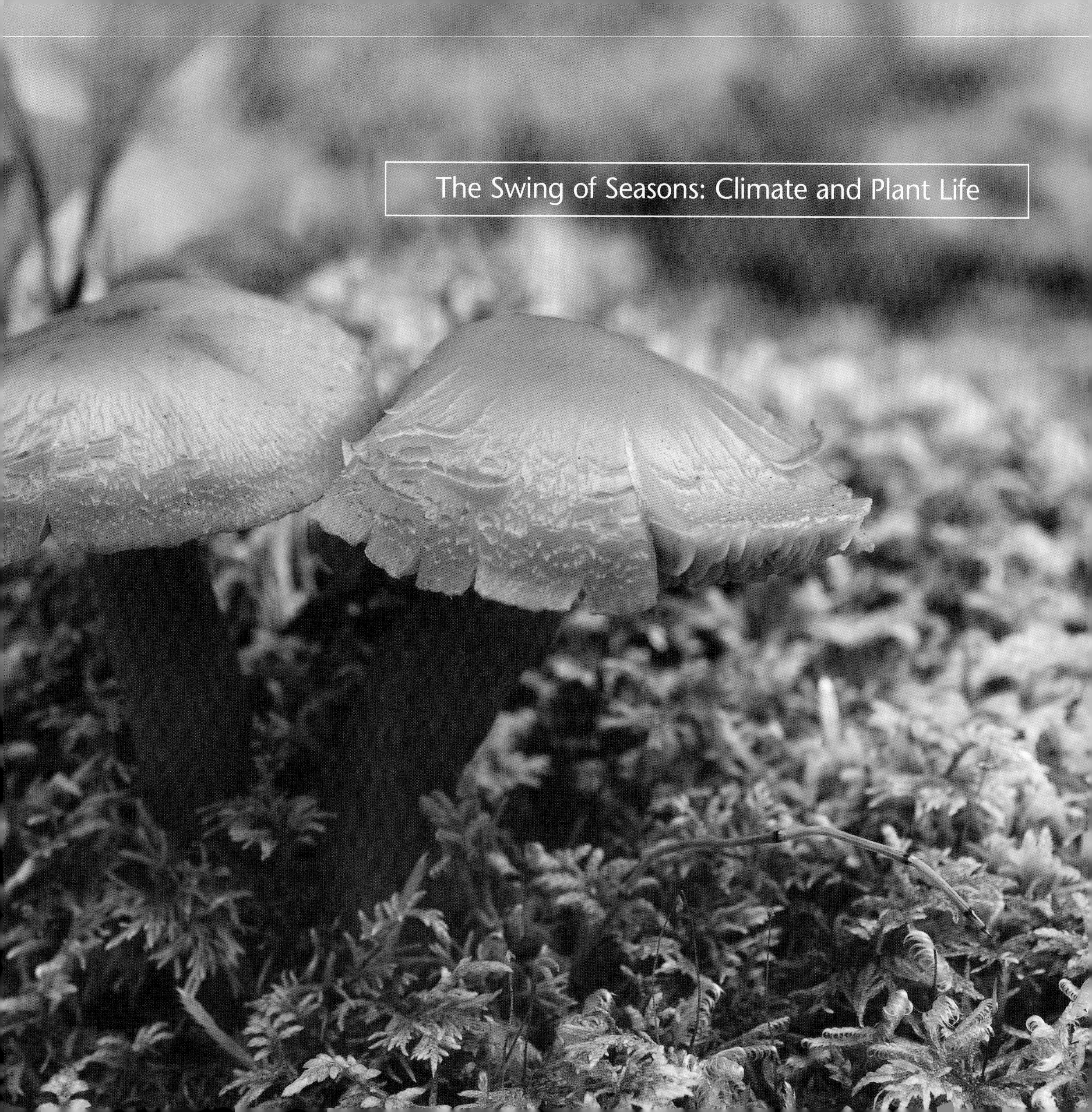

Well-suited for a winter landscape, a willow ptarmigan wears snowy, camouflaging plumage that includes leg- and foot-covering feathers. In spring, it will grow a mottled brown plumage.

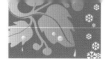

To the attentive eye, each moment of the year has its own beauty… it beholds, every hour, a picture which has never been seen before, and which shall never be seen again.

— Ralph Waldo Emerson

In the depths of a long, cold Denali winter, night lasts close to 20 hours. Even during so-called day, blue shadows haunt Subarctic Alaska, painting every crevice in the windblown snow. In December, when only the dancing northern lights offer colorful relief to a stoical, frozen land, it can be hard to imagine summer ever returning.

But after about seven snowy months, return it does—nudging brief, late spring out of the way to make time for a frenetic season of blooming flowers, swelling berries, buzzing insects, and the migrating birds they attract.

The Earth's tilt creates our seasons, directing the northern hemisphere away from the sun every winter and toward it every summer, with polar regions subjected to the greatest extremes—the longest nights for half the year, the longest days the other half. Spring and fall are the swing seasons when one extreme must transition quickly to the other. As the sun returns, it does so with astonishing and recognizable speed. Each day in the park between the winter and summer solstices, daylight increases between about four to six-and-a-half minutes. In a week, that adds up to an observable one-half to three-quarters of an hour of increasing light.

As winter progresses through brief spring and into busy summer, the sun's arc changes. Every day, it rises farther north, and crosses higher in the sky. By midsummer, for all but a few hours each day, the sun appears not to rise or set, but only to circle, from northeast to northwest. (Above the Arctic Circle, 200 miles north of Denali, the sun doesn't rise in mid-winter or set in mid-summer at all.)

If time seems to stand still in the seasonless tropics, it swings wildly at the high latitudes, reminding the visitor that no day is like any other and life is a race won by the fittest and the best-adapted—including the park's assemblage of 1,500 vascular plants, mosses, and lichens.

Taiga and Tundra

Denali's vegetated landscape is roughly divided into taiga, or northern boreal forest, and tundra, a treeless area. Taiga circles the northern parts of the globe, from Alaska to northern Canada, Scandinavia to

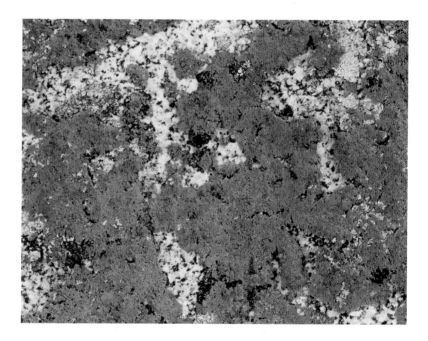

Lichens

Lichens aren't one species but two, a fungal host and alga—living as one. It appears in a variety of miniature shapes—bushy, scaly, or cup-like. Caribou consume lichen in great quantities; birds use it to line their nests. Like mosses, lichens don't have roots. When water is available, lichen absorbs it. When it's not, lichen shrivels, entering a state of dormancy. Thus protected from the vagaries of weather and climate, an individual lichen can survive to an ancient age—more than a thousand years, by some estimates.

Siberia. In the park, it cloaks lower elevations, including the park entrance area and more protected river valleys. Only eight species of trees occur in the park. Black spruce and white spruce are the most common, but the park also has pockets of larch, black cottonwood, Kenai birch, Alaska birch, balsam poplar, and quaking aspen.

Black spruce trees are well adapted to marginal northern environments and can grow where little else will. Its roots are shallow enough to grow in less than ten inches of cold, nutrient-poor, acidic soil.

The boggy aspects of this waterlogged soil deserve special mention. Interior Alaska is a near-desert. In other words, it's hard on well-exposed plants because it's too dry. But it's just as hard on some plants and trees in low-lying areas because it's too wet. Short summers don't allow much time for surface water to evaporate. Discontinuous permafrost—pockets of frozen ground—interferes with vertical drainage.

Permafrost also plays havoc with a slow-growing spruce's attempts to stand tall. Due to shallow soils over permafrost a grove of spindly black spruce trees may lean at odd angles, giving the appearance of poorly planted pipe cleaners.

Around the world few trees grow where the July temperature averages less than 50 degrees. In the park, treeline occurs at about 2,700 feet, with a considerable variation from place to place, depending on sun exposure and other factors.

Above treeline, stunted trees give way to two kinds of tundra. Shrub tundra—thick with knee-high willow, dwarf birch, and blueberry shrubs—blankets protected areas and lower elevations. Alpine tundra is easier to hike. It's found in higher and more exposed areas. Both kinds of tundra can grow in close proximity, forming a patchwork of shrubs, wildflowers, lichen, and mosses. This multicolored carpet, mostly green in summer, blazes countless shades of scarlet, mustard, and orange when fall arrives in August.

Plant Adaptations

Tundra plants are impressive survivors in this realm of extremes. What they need most—light—they receive in a concentrated three-month dose. Some low-growing evergreen plants can continue photosynthesizing from beneath a foot of snow, using the dim light that penetrates the snowpack.

Perennial plants fare best in Denali. Since snowmelt yields to summer practically overnight, plants prepare for it long in advance, developing buds for one to three years. When conditions are right, those buds can quickly burst into color. Purple mountain saxifrage, an alpine perennial that clings to moist crevices and loose scree, can flower from 5 to 16 days after snowmelt.

Even in summer, cold, dry, windy conditions are the norm for exposed tundra plants. Adaptive shapes and features help them cope. The woolly lousewort has fine, insulating hairs that shield the young plant from abrasive wind. Some plants grow year after year without shedding their leaves, creating a cozy moat of dead material. Low-growing plants take advantage of the warmer microclimate found just centimeters above the ground. They grow in mats,

It can be tricky packing for a trip to a park with unpredictable weather. The average July temperature is 55 degrees, but extreme variation is possible at any time of the year. In August 1984, a sudden storm dropped as much as ten inches of snowfall in parts of the park, with drifts of up to five feet forming. At the other end of the thermometer, a high of 91 degrees was recorded on June 22, 1991. Winter conditions are no less variable. The average January temperature is 2 degrees. The coldest temperature ever recorded at Park Headquarters was on February 5, 1999, when the mercury plunged to -54 degrees.

Treeline on the March

Researchers are keeping an eye on shifting white spruce treelines, a result of documented increases in park temperatures since 1976. The encroachment of spruce into higher elevations may reduce habitats for some tundra dwellers and limit wildlife views. Other warming impacts may include the invasion of shrubs into tundra, and shrinking ponds and lakes.

mounds, cushions and rosettes, minimizing their exposure to the elements, and placing their odds on living long, rather than growing tall.

There are exceptions, of course. Some plants make a compromise between short and tall, by keeping some parts close to the warm earth, and other parts high. Pallas's wallflower has ground-hugging tiny flowers, but its long, thin seed pods rise high above the rest of the plant, beckoning the wind for a ride across the windy, rocky slopes. One leggy plant, the arctic poppy, has bright-yellow, cup-shaped flowers that rotate daily like satellite dishes, in order to face the sun. The sun-warmed flowers offer an inviting place for insects to linger, increasing the poppy's chances for pollination.

All life turns toward the forces and elements that sustain it. Roots reach for water; lichens spread across and break down stone, plants cling to the warm earth or reach high toward wind and sky. The round, yellow poppy—a mirror image of the sun—constantly turns to face its energy source. At any given moment, a vast landscape such as Denali's may appear still, but that stillness is an illusion. Summer days may be long, but summer itself is short. Every living thing hurries to take advantage of ephemeral heat and light before winter comes again. ■

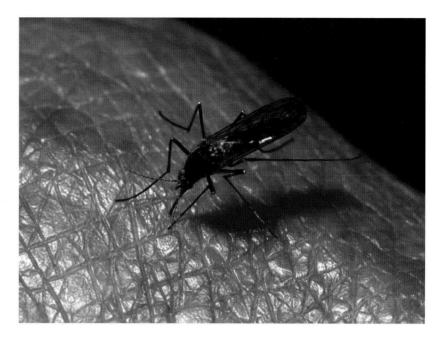

Insects

Mosquitoes and various species of biting or burrowing flies can send harried caribou fleeing to windy ridges and snowfields, where the annoying insects are at a disadvantage. But the buzzing pests have a welcome place in the park, too—both as a food source for birds and as a plant pollinator.

Black Spruce and Fire

Boy Scouts couldn't build a better tinder pile. Thin-barked and lichen-covered, with drooping lower branches, the black spruce is nature's perfect fire-maker—easy to ignite, quick to burn and die. But following that fiery death, black spruce regenerates at top speed. Fire opens the cones, allowing viable seeds to scatter. According to one study, four times as many black spruce seeds were dispersed in a recently burned area than in an unburned control. Birch and aspen also regenerate quickly in the wake of recurring fires.

In addition to scattering seeds, fire serves a house-cleaning function in black spruce forests, where thick layers of feather mosses and other organic materials accumulate on the forest floor, faster than nature's decomposers can handle. That buildup lowers the temperature of the forest floor, bringing permafrost closer to the surface. A fire reverses the process, clearing vegetation, warming soils, and dispersing nutrients previously tied up in dead, cold layers. While seldom seen by visitors, large wildfires periodically race across the dry, northern reaches of the park and have been a key component of the Denali ecosystem for thousands of years.

Perpetual Motion: Wildlife

The movement of things on this earth has always impressed me. There is a reassuring vitality in the annual rise of a river, in the return of the Arctic sun, in the poleward flight of spring migrations, in the seasonal trek of nomadic peoples.

— **John Haines**

The golden eagle soars above the tundra slope, the feathered edges of its six-foot wingspan splayed like fingers feeling the wind. Tilting its wings into a sharper V, the eagle makes a sudden dive toward prey. On the tundra slopes below, an arctic ground squirrel rushes for the cover of its burrow.

Everywhere the eagle flies, it energizes life in its shadow. Hoary marmots, snowshoe hares, and ptarmigan all flee from it. Even young Dall sheep skitter closer to their mothers in response to the beat of heavy wings. Golden eagles eat these species and many more. The remains of many Denali terrestrial vertebrates have been found in eagle nests.

The golden eagle's springtime aerial acrobatics—and its "take-no-prisoners" diet—are remarkable. But these vigorous displays are nothing compared to what the golden eagle and many other birds accomplish before arriving in the park. More than four-fifths of Denali birds are migrants, and they come from nearly every corner of the globe: Sandhill cranes from Texas and California. American golden plovers from Argentina and Uruguay. Northern wheatears from Africa. Long-tailed jaegers from the southern Pacific Ocean.

Some birds, like the golden eagle and the arctic tern, nest in Denali; others pass through en route to and from nesting grounds further north. To draw a picture of these birds' migration paths converging upon the park is to realize that Denali is not the edge of the world, but one of its pulsing centers, connecting Interior Alaska to just about every place on the planet.

Four-footed Wanderings

Other animals may not travel as far or as fast as the birds, but they all hurry through the Denali year, endeavoring to eat and to avoid being eaten, to outwit the elements, to prepare for the next winter as soon as the last has ended.

Caribou and Dall sheep are both herd animals that migrate within the park's borders. That movement can be horizontal—from one corner of the park to another, for example. But it is also vertical—a seasonal climb to higher areas, away from predators, or to cooler ridges with fewer biting pests.

Caribou numbers in Denali have fluctuated greatly this century, from a high of over 20,000 animals in the 1920s, to a low of under 1,000 animals in the 1970s. The population climbed to about 3,200 in 1989, but extreme snowfalls in 1990-1993 reduced the herd by nearly a third. The Denali herd is the only barren-ground caribou herd of its size in North America that is not hunted. Populations here rise and fall naturally, with predation and winter weather taking the greatest toll on caribou.

Today, the Denali herd is about 2,000 animals strong. That makes it much smaller than enormous coastal plain herds. However, even a small herd wouldn't survive if it remained sedentary. By traveling through the year, these members of the deer family avoid overgrazing the sparse tundra.

For Dall sheep, which number about 2,500 in the park, the most important movement is up—into rocky terrain where they, rather than wolves, can negotiate the terrain most gracefully. As summer's warmth moves up the mountains, Dall sheep follow that line of rising green into high ridges, where they are usually seen as distant white dots.

Female sheep, called ewes, give birth and maintain close bonds with single lambs. The mothers will occasionally venture toward lower, gentler terrain to nibble green plants, but they'll usually

Like four-fifths of Denali's bird species, the long-tailed jaeger is a seasonal migrant that makes the long trek north each summer. Supremely graceful aerial hunters, jaegers nest on the tundra and patrol the open landscape for voles and other small rodents.

Young moose pack on weight at a rate of more than two pounds a day—faster than any other Denali animal. Moose mothers give birth to calves—frequently twins—in the spring. Only 10 to 15 percent of moose calves survive their first year. But death doesn't remove energy from the ecosystem, it just delivers it into the mouths of other voracious mammals, including wolves and bears.

leave their young lambs behind in the care of a female relative—just in case danger is lurking nearby. In winter, some Dall sheep will make longer migrations, from the Alaska Range to the Outer Range north of the Park Road, where foraging is possible in areas with less snow.

Eating Overtime

Moose, with their barrel-shaped bodies and twiggy legs, can seem ungainly. But when they do choose to run, they run with speed and use their high profiles to advantage, easily stepping over obstacles that would slow a wolf or bear. On uneven ground, a running moose can pass a horse easily. They're also powerful swimmers, able to submerge completely for close to a minute and paddle comfortably for miles.

During the autumn rut, moose demonstrate their speed and might in loud, intimidating confrontations. Bulls circle each other stiffly, tilting their immense antlers. As the sparring heats up, equally matched mature bulls will clash and clinch antlers, pushing until the weaker bull relents and withdraws. Injuries and even death are not uncommon.

But truth be known—and both fight and flight aside—moose are nearly always observed in far more sedentary postures: Half-submerged in a shallow pond. Or standing among willow bushes, with no more apparent cares than a domestic cow. Of all the large Denali mammals, moose are most likely to give the false impression that life in the wild is an idle affair.

Yet sloth has no meaning in this northern landscape. Animals that don't expend energy migrating nonetheless spend ample time and energy securing, and digesting, food. A moose that appears to be standing still is usually, upon closer inspection, engaged in the life-or-death activity of consuming calories. A moose that appears to be resting in earnest, with slim legs tucked under its enormous brown body, is ruminating, or processing the huge quantities of woody plants that miraculously sustain 900 to 1,500 pounds of living flesh.

Lynx–Hare Populations

In boreal forests around the northern world, hare populations regularly rise and fall, in 8 to 11 year cycles. In low years, two or three snowshoe hares may inhabit a square mile; in peak years, many hundreds of hares crowd the same terrain. Some interplay of food limitation and predation are thought to be the causes, but everything from disease, forest fires, and even sunspots have been implicated.

A hare population crash sends ripples through the Denali ecosystem, affecting many predators—not only lynx, but also golden eagles, coyotes, great horned owls, and goshawks. Other animals that don't feed on the hares are affected by their wild swings, as well. When hare densities are low, predators turn to other small mammals, including arctic ground squirrels and red squirrels, bringing those animal populations down. As predators decline and vegetation recovers, hares busy themselves bearing large, frequent litters of leverets (baby hares), sending the hare population soaring again.

Hibernation—or Not

Denali is well known for its hibernating animals, including hoary marmots, arctic ground squirrels, and bears. Both black and grizzly bears were once classified as "false hibernators" because, while their metabolic rate drops by half, their body temperature remains high—above 88 degrees—during winter slumber. More recently, bears have been classified by many researchers as "super-hibernators." Unlike smaller, less well-insulated mammals, bears don't have to wake up every few days to warm up, urinate, and eat. Yet at a sign of danger, bears can wake up quickly, thanks to their relatively toasty body temperatures.

More surprising than our changing understanding of hibernation is the fact that most Denali animals don't hibernate in the first place, by any definition of that term. Voles, lemmings, mice, pikas, and shrews spend their winters living a "subnivean" existence, huddling and caching food in tunnels under the snow. Small mammals store less fat and expend more energy per pound than large mammals, and their high metabolic rates necessitate nearly constant feeding. Shrews will die within hours if deprived of food. The smallest of Denali's six shrew species—aptly named the tiny shrew—was first documented in the park in 2002 and weighs less than a dime.

One study found that Denali moose spend about six hours each winter day foraging, and twice as long ruminating. In the process, they can consume 30 to 60 pounds of vegetation in a day. The exception is during the rut, when mature bull moose don't eat at all, exposing them to greater risk of winter starvation, as compared to cows and younger bulls.

All that eating doesn't leave much time for sleep, which might be just as well, since moose are generally solitary and can't rely on herd mates to notify them of a predator's stealthy approach. A Canadian study found that in wintertime, moose may doze only one to two hours each 24-hour day. Even with such constant efforts, and even when browse is plentiful, moose generally can't digest enough food to sustain their bulk all winter. They rely on fat reserves to make up for the deficit. Like many Denali animals, the moose greets spring a good deal thinner than it was in fall.

For all that they take, moose give back, too. Their urine and feces fertilize willow shrubs, helping stripped willow bounce back from heavy browsing. The new growth encourages moose to return to the same spot and browse heavily again. The feedback loop works —within limits. If that limit is exceeded, over browsed vegetation can lead to a moose population crash.

Feeding Frenzies

In his book about Alaska, *Coming into the Country*, John McPhee described the thrill of seeing a brown bear in its native habitat—and how that sense of excitement can spread, like ripples on a pond, encompassing far more than a single animal or a single moment in time. "The sight of the bear stirred me like nothing else the country could contain," he wrote. "What mattered was not so much the bear himself as what the bear implied. He was the predominant thing in that country, and for him to be in it at all meant that there had to be more country like it in every direction and more of the same kind of country all around that. He implied a world."

Caribou

Denali caribou spend most of each year moving between areas where they feed, breed, and calve. Along the Park Road, they're usually seen in small clusters of a few to 20 animals. In fall, larger groups congregate for breeding, then often migrate to and beyond wintering grounds in the park's northeast corner, where wind may blow areas free of snow.

Year after year, the urge to move proves stronger than any landscape obstacles. Using their large, concave hooves as paddles, caribou can swim across rivers; using them as snowshoes, caribou can walk with relative ease across the snow, their weight supported across the hooves' large, circular surface. Caribou also use their hooves as sharp-edged shovels to break through snow crusts and reach patches of lichen, an important winter food high in digestible carbohydrates.

In spring, caribou will brave deep snow and storm to reach higher elevations, where they calve in the hills on Mount McKinley's northern flanks. But even as the caribou travel, perils follow. Newborn caribou can walk within an hour and sprint a day or two later, but that isn't fast enough to evade all predators. Wolves, grizzly bears, and golden eagles all prey on young caribou. In normal years, just over half of caribou calves may survive their first summer. In one exceptionally snowy year, researchers estimated that 91 percent of caribou calves perished.

But snow does have its comforts. Alpine snowfields offer some relief from early summer's insect hordes. As insect populations wane, and the caribou's stores of body fat drop, the caribou are driven to move again, back to more lushly vegetated areas at lower latitudes.

McPhee was making not only a philosophical observation, but an accurate ecological one as well. Bears are for the most part solitary, and their territories, while overlapping, are large. A bear's presence speaks to the openness and vitality of an entire area, which in turn supports many other animals. Scientists call grizzly bears an "umbrella species," meaning the same conditions that support them provide healthy conditions for other species as well.

Grizzly bears demand large spaces in part because only those large spaces can support sufficient food. Like the wolf, they will prey on moose; in fact, bears account for half of all moose fatalities at Denali. But bears aren't strictly carnivores, they're omnivores. That means they are able to eat anything and lots of it, including roots, grasses, and sedges. From mid- to late summer, berries are an essential food source. Counting the seeds in scat left behind as one bear gorged, a researcher once estimated that a grizzly could eat 200,000 soapberries in a day. Extending that equation, the park's estimated 300 grizzly bears may eat over a billion berries every few weeks.

Still, one has to wonder how a bear can strip so many berries so successfully. Not content to poke through scat, scientists have monitored bears' front ends as well. They've found that bears only manage to eat about one to five berries per bite. But they can bite 60 to 120 times per minute. What's more, they "high-grade" as they eat. Rather than consume every last berry off every last bush, bears actively stroll as they chew, pursuing the easiest berries and leaving the others behind.

Scientists have a word for bears' berry binges: hyperphagia, or "excessive eating." Really, there's nothing excessive about it. Grizzly bears must think with their stomachs for most of their waking hours in order to store enough fat to last the long winter. Alaska's coastal brown bears dine on salmon—and grow much larger than their

Chickadee Studies

For a bird, staying in a cold place year-round might not seem the smartest choice. And yet northern adaptations seem positively linked in the life of the black-capped chickadee—one of Denali's relatively few non-migratory birds. To last the winter, chickadees must eat frequently, often gaining 8 to 10 percent of their body mass each day and losing it again by the following morning, following a long night of fat-fueled shivering. To ensure an ample supply of food, chickadees cache seeds, and other food items, relying on their memories to find the caches later. Laboratory studies suggest that a chickadee's hippocampus—an area associated with memory—actually increases in size as caching begins after the breeding season.

Interior cousins. In most of the park, by contrast, large salmon runs are non-existent, and a buffet of other foods, including small mammals, must compensate.

Arctic ground squirrels are a favorite grizzly snack. With a muscular shoulder hump and claws perfect for digging, a grizzly is tailor-made for excavating the small mammals from their burrows. More than one naturalist has observed mother grizzlies excavating ground squirrels with great determination, and refusing to share the savory prizes with disappointed cubs. To enjoy some of life's finer things, cubs must learn to hunt for themselves.

Frozen Frog

In a land of swift animals, the record for most still—and most strange— goes to the wood frog, Denali's only amphibian. With water permeable skin, the frog can't avoid literally freezing each winter. By the time ice content has made up two-thirds of its body weight, the frog's heart stops, its breathing ceases, and "the frog teeters on the very edge of life," in the words of Life in the Cold *author Peter Marchand. Spring thaw returns the frog to normal function in less than a day.*

Cannibalism is observed more frequently between bears than among any other group of mammals. The park's two species of bears deal with the threat differently. Black bear cubs, which live in forested areas, can scramble up trees to evade a predatory adult male bear. On the open tundra, there is no such escape. Instead, mother bears must offer protection. That may explain why Denali's tundra-dwelling grizzly bear cubs have evolved a reliance on their mothers for longer periods—three-and-a-half years or more, as compared to one-and-a-half years among forest-dwelling black bears.

Grizzly bears living in open areas are more easily spotted by park visitors. Shy, forest-dwelling black bears are less commonly seen, but they are sometimes glimpsed in the wooded front country or near Kantishna. Grizzlies are larger, 450 to 600 pounds for the males, while black bears are 200 to 400 pounds. Their profiles are different, too. A grizzly has a larger shoulder hump, sagging belly, and what is frequently called a "dish-shaped" face, with a concave muzzle more distinctly angled away from the forehead. Black bears have a straighter "Roman" nose continuous with the slope of the forehead.

The one characteristic that can't be relied upon for identification of either bear species is color. Most black bears have brown muzzles, and some are not black at all, but rather cinnamon or honey. White, cream, and straw-colored grizzly bears are not unusual. Adolph Murie once quipped that a sourdough, or old-timer, told him he'd seen a mother grizzly with three cubs—"one lemon, one orange, and a chocolate!"

Grizzly bears mate between May and July. But through a process called delayed implantation (also common to black bears, as well as wolverines), the fertilized egg does not take hold and begin growing until the bear enters its den, in late October. Bear cubs— usually twins—are born in January, when the sow is still hibernating. If a mother bear has not accumulated enough fat, implantation will not take place. In this way, the bear hedges it bets, saving its energy

About 100 wolves make up more than a dozen packs in the park. The two most frequently spotted are the Grant Creek and East Fork packs, near the park's eastern side. Burdened with young pups, a pack's movements may follow the shape of a spoked wheel, returning again and again to the hub, or den, to bring the pups food. In winter, when the pups have grown, the entire pack roams across a broader range, tailing caribou, encircling moose, climbing into higher Dall sheep territory. Highly intelligent and socially close-knit, wolves howl as a way to promote pack unity and to advertise the limits of their territories to others.

and reproductive potential for better years when food and shelter are more available.

    Anything that compromises the bear's food sources, from sudden habitat degradation to long-term climate change, can have a profound impact on this long-lived, slowly reproducing mammal. Like the wolf, it fears little. Also like the wolf, it remains sovereign only through its industrious exploitation of a sparse environment. What the wolf accomplishes through its feet, the bear accomplishes with its jaws. Each one survives from one Subarctic year to the next by the slimmest of margins. ■

Eagle Studies

Denali is home to the only long-term study of golden eagle ecology in the northern latitudes of North America. Since 1987, wildlife biologist Carol McIntyre has tracked the reproductive success of more than 60 golden eagle pairs annually. Golden eagles migrate to Denali in late winter. At that time, the availability of prey, including snowshoe hares and ptarmigan, may be critical to how many new eaglets are produced. Traveling by small helicopter, McIntyre visits all known nesting areas in late April or early May, to see if they are occupied and to document breeding activities. The nests are usually found on cliffs or rock outcroppings. She returns a second time in late July to check on young eagles preparing to fledge from their nests. McIntyre and cooperating scientists also use satellite radio telemetry to track transmitter-carrying eagles, to record their migratory routes and the many perils—from habitat loss to poaching—that threaten their survival far beyond Denali's borders.

First Peoples, First Conservationists

Athabascan Indians understood how to survive in a hungry land, where every season meant getting ready for the next. Flexibility in hunting and fishing, and the ability to roam far in small groups, were keys to making the most of meager resources.

Native Alaskans first passed this way more than 11,000 years ago. Today's park stands at the very heart of Athabascan country, where the activities of nomadic hunters and gatherers from five different groups—the Koyukon, Tanana, Ahtna, Tanaina, and Upper Kuskokwim—overlapped, without fixed boundaries. Each of these groups was further subdivided into bands, usually composed of two to five families. A band traveled between seasonal camps and a more permanent winter base, roaming a territory of some 2,500 square miles.

Collectively, bands drove caribou along specially erected fences and herded Dall sheep toward high areas where other hunters waited, ready to ambush the animals with spears and bows. Athabaskans also fished, but Denali's silty streams and small rivers don't have the large salmon runs that form the basis of traditional life in coastal Alaska. In a land of migrating animals and naturally fluctuating wildlife populations, diversity was essential—as was independence. In lean years, a small band could break down into even smaller households, able to wander far and opportunistically subsist. There was no concept of a large, political group beyond the regional band, and no recognition of leadership beyond that of an informal headman.

Athabascan Indians living in and just beyond the park's western corners, far from the coast and from large navigable rivers, had little direct contact with non-Natives until the nineteenth century. Contact brought an end to the nomadic lifestyle, but not an end to reliance on wild foods and the seasonal round.

The Alaska National Interest Lands Conservation Act (ANILCA) insured the rights of villagers from Cantwell, Lake Minchumina, Nikolai and Telida, and other individuals to conduct subsistence activities in the new park and preserve lands that were added to Denali in 1980. Writes Raymond Collins in his Nikolai-Telida Village History Report, "The park can be considered wilderness, not because it has been protected from human use, but because the people who used it for thousands of years did not attempt to change its basic nature."

Moved to Conserve: Park Pioneers

We need the tonic of wildness...
— Henry David Thoreau

It is possible to marvel at Denali National Park and Preserve from a distance, to be struck by the abstract ideal of untouched wilderness without ever seeing the wilderness itself. But the people who ended up having the strongest effect on this land in modern times were the ones who came, who walked and climbed, who took the time to study and search and listen, who grappled with the majesty and complexity of this place firsthand. Few of these people came with considerable expertise in the ecology of Subarctic environments; they gained that knowledge here. Few of them came with firmly preconceived notions about what wilderness is or how it should be saved; they shaped those notions here.

Charles Sheldon was the first person to propose making the area a game refuge. A native of Vermont, educated at Yale, he had made his name and fortune in the railroad business and was able to retire in 1903, at the age of 35. Hunting and natural history were his passions. In the style of Teddy Roosevelt, who would later pen a foreword to one of Sheldon's books, Sheldon devoted himself to pairing outdoor prowess with public service.

Following a trip to Mexico, where he developed an interest in mountain sheep, Sheldon was invited by the U.S. Biological Survey to visit the Denali area in 1906. His primary aim was to conduct a Dall sheep survey and gather ram specimens. His diaries confirm, however, that Sheldon's eye and heart roamed well beyond the cliffy haunts of a single trophy species.

Even after hiking for days without managing to bag or even spot sheep, Sheldon's spirits stayed high and he expressed his delight for all of Denali's wildlife. During a forced layover while his ankle was recovering from a painful carbuncle, Sheldon set traps for small mammals ("always so interesting to the faunal naturalist") and took notes on the diverse wildlife visible from camp: "The abundant ground squirrels amused us, marmots whistled on the moraine, Canada jays (called gray jays today) flew about, the tree sparrows and intermediate sparrows sang continually, and waxwings and northern shrikes were particularly plentiful. White-tailed ptarmigan with broods of chicks were near; the wing beats of ravens passing overhead hissed through the air; arctic terns flew gracefully over the meadows; and the golden eagles soared above the ridges."

Denali Sled Dogs

From the earliest days under first superintendent Karstens, sled dogs have added their hardworking energy to the park. First, they were the living engines that allowed rangers to put a stop to rampant poaching. Today, they're still used on winter patrols that last anywhere from a single day to six weeks. In total, the dogs log about 3,000 miles each winter as they help rangers make contact with visitors, assist researchers, and watch boundaries while maintaining the park's wilderness ethic. The historic Denali kennels are open to the public and sled dog demonstrations are a popular front country attraction.

Charles Sheldon, naturalist and hunter, visited the Denali region in 1906 to study Dall sheep and later suggested making the area a game refuge. Over 100 years later, park policy prohibits feeding wildlife so that animals remain wild.

He enthused just as readily about geologic features. Surveying the Peters Glacier for sheep one day without success, he decided to linger in order to marvel at the mountainous scenery. Ascending several thousand feet, he seated himself above the glacier, where he could watch a series of avalanches cascade down the glacier's snout and strike bare rock walls below. Crashing ice and swirling snow alternated with "supreme" silence during the four hours he spent there, watching 19 avalanches fall.

Sheldon returned to Alaska in 1907 and stayed nearly a year, observing wildlife through the seasons in the company of Harry Karstens, and overwintering in a cabin on the Toklat River. He filled notebooks with observations of animal migrations, matings, predation, and play. He also spent time pondering that wildlife's uncertain future, given the influx of miners and the inevitability of surrounding development. Together, he and Karstens lamented the waste created by local market hunters slaughtering vast numbers of wild sheep for sale as food to nearby towns and camps.

By the end of Sheldon's second stay, he and Karstens, who would later serve as the park's first superintendent, had imagined the role a game preserve could play in safeguarding this immense living landscape, and had even sketched potential boundary lines. With the help of other conservationists—and despite considerable opposition—an idea hatched in the wilderness became reality in 1917, when Congress passed a bill to establish Mount McKinley National Park.

Among the Wolves

Every bit as tireless as Sheldon and Karstens, scientist Adolph Murie has been called "the single most influential person" shaping the geography and wildlife policies of the modern park. Murie made his greatest contribution—and earned a reputation as Denali's "conscience"—in answer to a perceived crisis. A series of extreme winter snows 1929

and 1932 had taken their toll on the Dall sheep population, reducing it from an unusually high number, over 10,000 animals, to an alarmingly low count, about 1,000. Some of the same sportsmen's groups that had supported park creation now pressured the park for predator control. This meant wolf killing, and it came at a time when wolves were being purged from public lands across the country. The last wolves in Yellowstone had been killed in 1926.

Harry Karstens

The park was already four years old when a well-respected Alaska sourdough named Harry Karstens was given the task of protecting it, as the first superintendent. From 1921 to 1928, Karstens faced the enormous task of combating poaching, building a base camp, managing dog and horse teams, and dealing with early visitors who arrived by railroad expecting to find better tourism facilities—or a longer road than the one just beginning to penetrate the park in 1923. Karstens spoke proudly of the park's "beauty and grandeur," but also cautioned would-be tourists, "There is little to offer visitors… who would become hysterical about a few insects or faint and become panic stricken if they missed a meal or two."

Murie's 1939 to 1941 studies found that Dall sheep numbers, while low, appeared to be stable. Through firsthand observation, he found that wolves seemed to target the old and the weak. He suggested that predation might actually have a salutary effect on a population by removing the less-fit members of a species. He concluded that the National Park Service should not favor any one species over another—a hard line to draw, given Americans' great affection for the snow-white Dall sheep. Murie recommended that the park stop the limited wolf control already implemented in 1929. Strong feelings on both sides of the issue continued, and alarm about sheep populations a few years later raised the wolf question yet again. But predator control was ended for good in 1952.

By watching wolves and making notes of their family life, including displays of tenderness and intelligence, Murie began to counter negative stereotypes that had been entrenched at least since the Middle Ages. Murie managed to convey such information without romanticizing it or playing favorites. It's noteworthy that his landmark book, *The Wolves of Mount McKinley*, dedicates about 70 pages to wolves, and about 170 pages to other Denali animals, including Dall sheep, caribou, moose, bears, foxes, and golden eagles. In Murie's mind, it probably couldn't have been any other way. Through his fieldwork, he had seen how the lives of all those animals are intertwined.

Just as astounding as Murie's conclusions were the sheer physical efforts he made while studying all the park animals. He studied the remains of 829 sheep and peered into more than two-dozen eagle nests. When he wanted to know what animals ate, he dug into the evidence, analyzing the bone and feather residues in 1,174 wolf scats, 786 fox scats, and 632 eagle pellets. Most of all he walked—1,700 miles in 1939 alone—proving himself as tireless and enduring as the animals he studied.

Expanding the Park

Many park pioneers, planners, and users noted that the original Mount McKinley National Park, as grand and impressive as it was, did not encompass all that it could—or should. The peaks of great mountains, including the continent's highest summit, fell within park boundaries, but to the south, great gorges and glaciers fell

From a high vantage point above precarious cliffs, several wolves patiently scrutinize their prey, below. Modern studies have confirmed Adolph Murie's ideas: that wolves disproportionately target the old and the weak.

Celia Hunter

From the month in late 1946 when she weathered snowstorms to help ferry a war surplus plane from Seattle to Fairbanks, to the night before her death in December 2001, which she spent writing letters to her senators urging them to vote against proposed oil drilling in the Arctic National Wildlife Refuge, Celia Hunter never shied away from challenges. With her friend Ginny Hill Woods, a fellow Women Airforce Service Pilot, Hunter settled permanently in Alaska in 1949. In 1952, with Ginny's husband Morton Wood, a Denali park ranger, the women founded Camp Denali, a rustic tent camp (cabins were added later) that catered to some of Alaska first eco-tourists.

One fall, a bear destroyed several Camp Denali buildings. Hunter took the damage in stride, informing readers of her camp newsletter, "This is what we like about Alaska. The land, the climate, the elements are neither for you nor against you. They are just there, and how you measure up to the challenge of coping with them is the true measure of yourself…."

In addition to serving park visitors for decades, Hunter gained renown as an environmentalist, founding the Alaska Conservation Society and becoming, as executive director of The Wilderness Society, the first woman to lead a national environmental organization. A lifelong Denali advocate who was instrumental in the park's 1980 expansion, Celia Hunter wrote just before her death at the age of 82, "Don't become despondent because those at the top show no signs of understanding the global crisis or any real concern about solving the basic problems. The solution will come from the work and interconnections of people working where they live to keep their ties with the earth and its natural systems and with all the creatures that share this home with us. We have much to learn, but it is not too late."

Visitors help protect Denali by riding tour and shuttle buses, a mandatory system established in 1972 to minimize traffic and reduce impacts to the environment. As an added benefit, visitors have up to 51 pairs of eyes to help them look for wildlife and a knowledgeable driver to answer questions. Access for private vehicles is controlled beyond the Savage River checkpoint, at mile 15. For those who want to see the backcountry away from the 92-mile Denali Park Road, there are a limited number of marked trails, and even more opportunities to hike trailless wilderness areas.

outside the boundary. Animals paid no more attention to the park's original rectangular outline than glaciers did. In 1963, consulting naturalist Sigurd Olson reported that the park's "boundaries cut across normal game habitats irrespective of migration routes or breeding requirements."

In Fairbanks, members of an association called the Pioneers of Alaska called for park additions to protect wintering ranges to the north and prime sheep habitat to the west. Celia Hunter and Ginny Hill Wood, founders of Camp Denali —a wilderness camp just north of the original park boundary—proposed a buffer to protect wildlife and views in the Wonder Lake area.

In the late 1960s, calls for park expansion became just one piece in a larger state land issues puzzle. The Statehood Act of 1958 had granted Alaska the right to select 104 million acres of the state's 375-million-acre total to be used as its economic and natural resource base. These selections were frozen in 1966, however, pending resolution of Native land-claims issues.

The 1968 discovery of oil at Prudhoe Bay in northern Alaska added pressure to resolve the stalemate. Until long-contested Native land issues were settled, the state couldn't build an overland pipeline that would deliver arctic oil to an ice-free port in southern Alaska. In 1971, Congress enacted the Alaska Native Claims Settlement Act, giving Alaska's Natives the right to select 44 million acres of land. Under pressure from conservationists, Congress also required federal agencies to recommend public lands for inclusion in parks, wildlife refuges, wild and scenic rivers, and forests. Nine more years of negotiations followed before the Alaska National Interest Lands Conservation Act (ANILCA) of 1980 was passed.

ANILCA set aside 106 million acres of conservation units in Alaska, including the four million acres added to Mount McKinley National Park, tripling its size. Renamed Denali National Park and

Preserve, the six-million-acre unit now encompasses the old park as well as new park and preserve lands where both traditional subsistence and sport hunting and fishing are allowed. The expanded park fulfills the early park pioneers' vision of a vast protected landscape, large enough to encompass both grand geological features and intricate ecosystems.

Our Role in Denali's Future

Most of today's park visitors won't wear out as many boots as Murie; won't ride a park ranger's dog-sled through miles of frozen winter wilderness in pursuit of poachers; or stand, as Sheldon did, perilously close to avalanches. But each moment in the park brings us closer to

our own understanding of, and appreciation for, this dynamic place.

We are moved by the wildlife and landscape we see; and just as often, moved by a glimpse of wilderness that suggests life and open space beyond our own sight and reach. As Henry David Thoreau wrote, "We need the tonic of wildness … We need to witness our own limits transgressed, and some life pasturing freely where we never wander."

That witnessing can inspire us to continue caring about Denali National Park and Preserve, and acting on its behalf, even after we've returned home.

Early conservationists recognized the need for a park. Denali advocates of the 1960s and 1970s recognized that only expanded borders would serve the wildlife and geographical features that decades of park visitors had come to love. Perhaps it is our generation's task to realize that even those expanded borders are not sufficient; that the future of Denali wildlife is linked to larger global concerns.

Science now informs us that habitat changes thousands of miles away affect Denali's migratory birds; that environmental contaminants find their way into Denali waters; that climate change will affect this place just as it will affect many sensitive places around the world. The positive changes we make on behalf of these global issues will benefit Denali, too, allowing this wilderness to move hearts and minds for generations to come. ■

Sampling of Species

Trumpeter swan	*Cygnus buccinator*
Harlequin duck	*Histrionicus histrionicus*
Willow ptarmigan	*Lagopus leucura*
White-tailed ptarmigan	*Lagopus leucretus*
Golden eagle	*Aquila chrysaetos*
Gyrfalcon	*Falco rusticolus*
Sandhill crane	*Grus canadensis*
American golden-plover	*Pluvialis dominica*
Long-tailed jaeger	*Stercorarius longicaudus*
Arctic tern	*Sterna paradisaea*
Boreal owl	*Aegolius funereus*
Black-capped chickadee	*Poecile atricapillus*
Boreal chickadee	*Poecile hudsonica*
Arctic warbler	*Phylloscopus borealis*
Northern wheatear	*Oenanthe oenanthe*
Bohemian waxwing	*Bombycilla garrulus*
Blackpoll warbler	*Dendroica striata*
White-winged crossbill	*Loxia leucoptera*
Black spruce	*Picea mariana*
White spruce	*Picea glauca*
Quaking aspen	*Populus tremuloides*
Alaska birch	*Betula neoalaskana*
Blueberry	*Vaccinium uliginosum*
Highbush cranberry	*Viburnum edule*
Dwarf dogwood	*Cornus canadensis*
Arctic lupine	*Lupinus arctians*
Fireweed	*Epilobium angustifolium*
Wild geranium	*Geranium erianthum*
Alpine forget-me-not	*Myosotis alpestris*
Yellow pond lily	*Nuphar polysepalum*

Large flocks of the graceful sandhill crane stop in Denali during migration. Clockwise from top right: Arctic lupine, trumpeter swan with cygnets, blueberries.

Sampling of Species

Tundra shrew	*Sorex tundrensis*
Little brown bat	*Myotis lucifugus*
Coyote	*Canis latrans*
Gray wolf	*Canis lupus*
Red fox	*Vulpes vulpes*
Lynx	*Lynx canadensis*
Northern river otter	*Lontra canadensis*
Wolverine	*Gulo gulo*
Ermine	*Mustela erminea*
American black bear	*Ursus americanus*
Brown bear	*Ursus arctos*
Moose	*Alces alces*
Caribou	*Rangifer tarandus*
Dall sheep	*Ovis dalli*
Hoary marmot	*Marmota caligata*
Arctic ground squirrel	*Spermophilus parryii*
Red squirrel	*Tamiasciurus hudsonicus*
Northern flying squirrel	*Glaucomys sabrinus*
American beaver	*Castor canadensis*
Northern red-backed vole	*Myodes rutilus*
Brown lemming	*Lemmus trimucronatus*
Singing vole	*Microtus miurus*
Tundra vole	*Microtus oeconomus*
Taiga vole	*Microtus xanthognathus*
Muskrat	*Ondatra zibethicus*
Northern bog lemming	*Synaptomys borealis*
N. American porcupine	*Erethizon dorsatum*
Collared pika	*Ochotona collaris*
Snowshoe hare	*Lepus americanus*

Dall sheep use ridges and steep slopes for feeding and resting, and rocky, craggy areas to elude predators. Clockwise from top right: collared pika, moose, beaver.

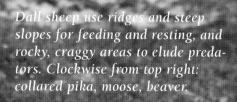